Why Am I a Reptile?

Greg Pyers

Raintree

Chicago, Illinois

© 2006 Raintree
a division of Reed Elsevier Inc.
Chicago, Illinois

Customer Service 888-363-4266
Visit our website at www.raintreelibrary.com

For information, address the publisher:
Raintree, 100 N. LaSalle, Suite 1200, Chicago, IL 60602

Typeset in 21/30 pt Goudy Sans Book
Printed and bound in China by South China
Printing Company Ltd

10 09 08 07 06
10 9 8 7 6 5 4 3 2 1

Library of Congress Cataloging-in-Publication Data
Pyers, Greg.
  Why am I a reptile? / Greg Pyers.
      p. cm. -- (Classifying animals)
  Includes index.
  ISBN 1-4109-2017-8 (library binding-hardcover) --
  ISBN 1-4109-2024-0 (pbk.)
  1. Reptiles--Juvenile literature. I. Title.
  QL644.2.P94 2006
  597.9--dc22
                          2005012258

Acknowledgments
The author and publishers are grateful to the following for permission to reproduce copyright material: APL/Corbis/© Nik Wheeler: p. **12**, /© George D. Lepp: p. **13**, /© Kevin Schafer: p. **26**; © Joe McDonald/ Visuals Unlimited: p. **27**; Wendell Metzen/Bruce Coleman Images: p. **18**; Steven David Miller/Auscape International: p. **24**; Naturepl.com/ Barry Mansell: p. **21**, /Adrian Davies: p. **23**; Photolibrary.com/Peter Arnold: pp. **4**, **9**, **20**, /AnimalsAnimals: pp. **6–7**, **16–17**, /OSF: pp. **8**, **14**, **22**, **25**; Skulls Unlimited: p. **10**. All other images PhotoDisc.

Cover photograph of an American alligator is reproduced with permission of Photolibrary.com/OSF.

Every effort has been made to contact copyright holders of any material reproduced in this book. Any omissions will be rectified in subsequent printings if notice is given to the publisher.

The paper used to print this book comes from sustainable resources.

Contents

Words that are printed in bold, **like this**, are explained in the glossary on page 31.

All Kinds of Animals

There are millions of different kinds of animals. There are big animals, small animals, furry animals, and feathered animals. There are animals that swim and animals that fly. There are even some animals that look like plants!

But you have probably noticed that, despite all these differences, some animals are still rather similar to one another.

A snake is a long, thin animal with no legs.

Sorting

We sort clothes into different drawers and shelves to help us find the right ones when we need them. Animals that are similar to one another can also be sorted into groups. Sorting animals into different groups can help us learn about them. This sorting is called **classification**.

This chart shows one way that we can sort animals into groups. Vertebrates are animals with backbones. Invertebrates are animals without backbones. Reptiles are vertebrates.

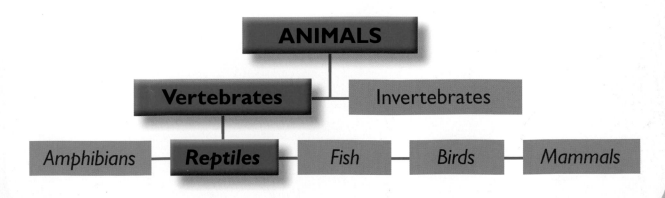

An Alligator Is a Reptile

Reptiles are one group of animals. There are 6,300 different **species**, or kinds, of reptiles. Snakes, lizards, turtles, and crocodiles are reptiles. But why? What makes a reptile a reptile? In this book, we will look closely at one reptile, the American alligator, to find out.

FAST FACT

The world's largest reptile is the saltwater crocodile. It can grow to more than 19.7 feet (6 meters) long and weigh 2,205 pounds (1,000 kilograms).

As you read through this book, you will see a ✓ next to important information that tells you what makes a reptile a reptile.

An American alligator may grow to 13 feet (4 meters) long and weigh more than 550 pounds (250 kilograms).

Crocodilians

The American alligator belongs to a group of reptiles called **crocodilians**. Alligators, crocodiles, gavials, and caimans are crocodilians. All crocodilians live in **wetland habitats** in warm, **tropical** parts of the world.

Predators

Crocodilians are **predators**. When it is very young, an American alligator hunts for small **prey**, such as frogs. As it grows, it eats larger prey, such as deer. Young alligators are often eaten by older alligators.

An American alligator sometimes hunts great egrets.

An Alligator's Body

An American alligator's body is long and heavy. ✔ Like all reptiles with limbs, an American alligator's four legs stick out from the sides of its body, not underneath. With legs like these, the alligator sways when it walks. Walking causes it to get tired quickly.

An American alligator's legs cannot support its heavy body for very long.

Scales

✅ Like all reptiles, an American alligator is covered in **scales**. These fit together like bricks in a path. But not all the scales are the same shape or size. The scales on the alligator's back are hard and rough. These protect the alligator if it gets into a fight. The scales on an American alligator's belly are flat, soft, and smooth. These help the alligator slide easily from a muddy bank into the water.

An American alligator has large scales on its back and smaller scales on its sides.

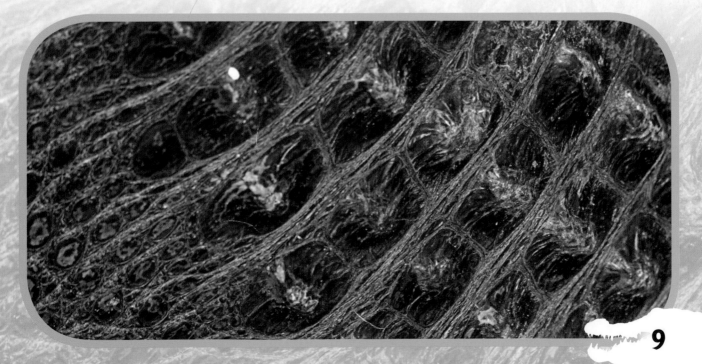

9

Inside an Alligator

Inside an American alligator is a skeleton of bones. Covering the skeleton is a layer of muscles. Covering the muscles is the alligator's **scaly** skin.

Backbone

Running along an American alligator's back is a backbone. The backbone is actually made up of many small bones joined together. The alligator's leg bones, tail bones, **skull**, and ribs are attached to the backbone. ✔ All reptiles have a skeleton and a backbone inside their body.

An American alligator has a skeleton inside its body.

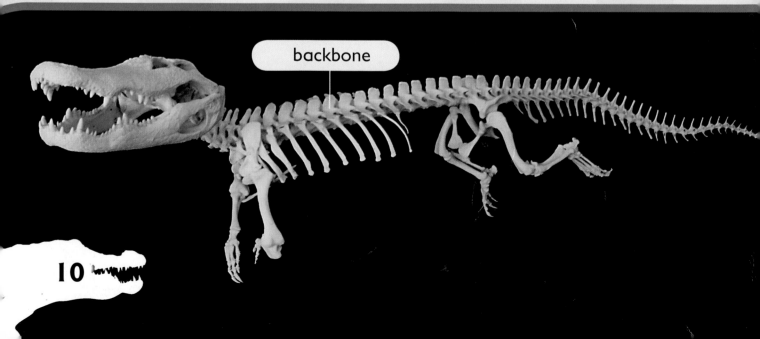

backbone

Organs

There are **organs** inside an American alligator. These include a heart, a liver, a stomach, and **lungs**. The organs have important jobs to do.

Breathing

An American alligator's lungs take in **oxygen** from the air. When the alligator breathes through its nose or mouth, air moves into the alligator's lungs. From there, oxygen passes into the blood. ✓ All reptiles have lungs and breathe air.

These are some of the organs inside an American alligator.

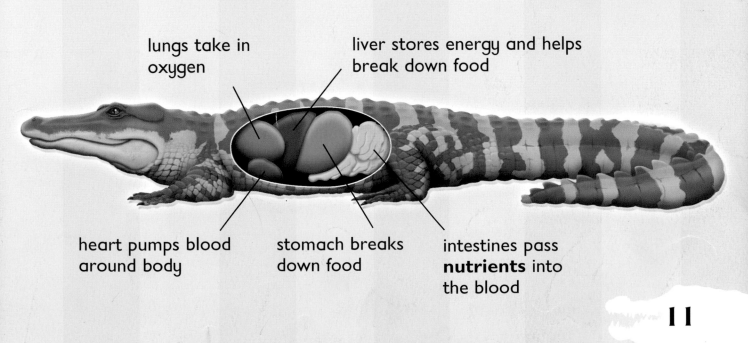

lungs take in oxygen

liver stores energy and helps break down food

heart pumps blood around body

stomach breaks down food

intestines pass **nutrients** into the blood

Getting Warm

Like all reptiles, American alligators need the sun to warm their bodies. On a cold day, a reptile's body will be cold. This is why reptiles are often called cold-blooded animals. But on a warm day, a reptile's body will be warm.

FAST FACT

Most reptiles live in warm parts of the world. This is because they need the sun to warm themselves up.

An American alligator's dark color helps it to soak up the sun's heat quickly.

Being active

An American alligator must have a warm body so that it can hunt and swim. To warm up, the alligator lies in a sunny place out of the water. In winter, American alligators cannot warm up at all. At that time of year, they often bury themselves in mud and stay there until warm weather comes in spring.

If an American alligator gets too warm, it cools down by moving into the shade or slipping into the water.

Food

American alligators are carnivores. This means that they eat other animals. Fish, turtles, snakes, and birds are some of the animals an American alligator hunts. These animals are the alligator's **prey**.

An American alligator also hunts deer.

14

Hunting

An American alligator swims silently when it is hunting. It sweeps its tail from side to side. It steers with its back feet. Its back feet are **webbed**. If a deer comes to the water's edge to drink, the alligator disappears below the water's surface. It swims closer and closer. At the last moment, it lunges from the water and grabs the deer in its powerful jaws. It holds tight with its teeth and drags its prey into the water.

Only the alligator's eyes and nostrils can be seen above the water as it waits for prey.

Feeding

An American alligator kills its **prey** by drowning it or by tearing it apart with its teeth. An alligator's jaws are strong enough to crush bones. An American alligator does not chew its food. Instead, it swallows its food in large chunks.

An American alligator has strong jaws, sharp teeth, and a mouth that opens wide.

Stomach stones

Like all animals, an American alligator needs **nutrients** to survive. An American alligator gets these nutrients by breaking its food down into tiny pieces. This happens in its stomach. An American alligator swallows stones, which then sit in its stomach. These help to grind up the food. The nutrients then pass into the blood. The blood carries the nutrients around the alligator's body.

Winter

In winter, it is too cold for an American alligator to hunt. It survives on its body fat, which is stored from food eaten over the warmer months.

An American alligator's body fat is mostly stored around the middle of its body.

Communication

American alligators **communicate** with sounds. They make more sounds than any other **crocodilian**. They growl when they fight. They hiss as a warning not to come near. American alligators also make grunts to call their young. Young alligators make a "yipping" sound to call their mother when they hatch from their eggs.

American alligators also communicate with body signals. An alligator may open its mouth, puff up its body, and stand tall as a warning to other alligators or people not to come near.

American alligators growl to communicate with one another in the water.

Mating time

American alligators are noisiest in spring. At that time of year, male alligators and female alligators come together to **mate**. The alligators bellow. This loud, deep sound brings more alligators together. Male alligators also make a sound so low we cannot hear it. They make this sound to tell other males to stay away.

An American alligator bellows to call other alligators at mating time.

Nesting

Different reptiles have different life cycles. A female American alligator builds a nest after **mating**. She piles leaves, grass, and sticks together, then lays about 40 eggs in the center. The female alligator then covers her eggs with leaves.

The female American alligator builds a nest 6.6 feet (2 meters) across and 3.3 feet (1 meter) high.

Keeping the eggs warm

As the leaves in the nest rot, they give off heat. The heat keeps the eggs warm. This is called **incubation**. Inside each egg, an alligator baby begins to grow. At this stage it is called an **embryo**. If the nest is hot, the embryos will become males. If the **temperature** is warm, they will become females. If the temperature is in between, some males and some females will hatch.

Each American alligator egg has a white shell and is about the size of a chicken's egg.

Hatching

The female American alligator guards her nest and eggs from **predators**. After about two months, the baby American alligators begin to hatch from the eggs. They call, "Yip, yip." The mother hears them and opens the nest. Gently, she uses her teeth to crack open any unhatched eggs.

Baby American alligators look similar to the **adults** when they hatch.

Mother's protection

The baby American alligators are called hatchlings. They are small and helpless and need protection. They cannot defend themselves against predators, such as hawks, snakes, or other alligators. The mother picks up the hatchlings in her mouth and carries them to the water. She will watch over them for the next year or two.

FAST FACT

Most reptile babies have to take care of themselves when they hatch. After a green turtle has laid her eggs, she returns to the sea. When her babies hatch, they have to find their own way.

Baby American alligators stay near their mother for protection.

Growing Up

When they hatch, American alligators are just 6 inches (15 centimeters) long. At six years of age they are 6.6 feet (2 meters) long. When they are small, the young alligators eat small animals. This **prey** includes frogs, tadpoles (young frogs and toads), snails, and insects. As the alligators become bigger, they eat bigger prey.

Young American alligators grow quickly.

FAST FACT

The Aldabra giant tortoise is a reptile that grows slowly. It takes 40 years to reach its full weight of 353 pounds (160 kilograms). The oldest known Aldabra giant tortoise lived to be 152 years old.

Dangers

Young American alligators are eaten by many **predators**. These include large fish, herons, turtles, snakes, and black bears. This is why young alligators keep out of sight among the waterweeds in shallow water.

When the young alligators are two years old, their mother no longer protects them. By then, they are almost big enough to be safe from most predators. When they are fully grown, no predator can harm them. Alligators were once hunted by humans, but today hunting is no longer allowed. An American alligator may live for 50 years or more.

Young American alligators stay together among the waterweeds.

Is It a Reptile?

An American alligator is a reptile because:

- ✓ It has a backbone
- ✓ It has **lungs** and breathes air
- ✓ Its body is covered in **scales**
- ✓ It needs the sun's warmth to heat up its body
- ✓ Its limbs are attached to the sides of its body.

An American alligator is a reptile.

Test yourself: tokay gecko

This animal gets its name from the "tok-ay" call the males make. After **mating**, the female tokay gecko lays eggs. She protects her eggs fiercely by barking at any animal that comes too close. Tokay geckos have a backbone and breathe air. They have soft, scaly skin. They need the sun to warm up their bodies. A tokay gecko's four legs are attached to the sides of its body. This helps it to lie flat against branches and tree trunks, out of sight of **predators**.

Is the tokay gecko a reptile? You decide. (You will find the answer at the bottom of page 30.)

Tokay geckos live in forests in Madagascar, which is a hot country.

Animal Groups

This table shows the main features of the animals in each animal group.

Mammals	Birds	Reptiles
backbone	backbone	backbone
skeleton inside body	skeleton inside body	skeleton inside body
most have four limbs	four limbs	most have four limbs
breathe air with **lungs**	breathe air with lungs	breathe air with lungs
most have hair or fur	all have feathers	all have **scales**
most born live; three **species** hatch from eggs; females' bodies make milk to feed young	all hatch from eggs with hard shells	many hatch from eggs with leathery shells; many born live
steady, warm body **temperature**	steady, warm body temperature	changing body temperature

Fish	Amphibians	Insects
backbone	backbone	no backbone
skeleton inside body	skeleton inside body	exoskeleton outside body
most have fins	most have four limbs	six legs
all have gills	gills during first stage; **adults** breathe air with lungs	breathe air but have no lungs
most have scales	no feathers, scales, or hair	many have some hair
most hatch from eggs; some born live	all hatch from eggs without shells	many hatch from eggs; many born live
changing body temperature	changing body temperature	changing body temperature

Find Out for Yourself

To see an American alligator in the wild, you will have to visit Florida, Louisiana, or Texas. Many zoos across the United States also have these animals, as well as other kinds of reptiles, for you to look at. Perhaps there are reptiles in your garden or local park that you could watch.

For more information about alligators and other reptiles, you can read more books and look on the Internet.

More books to read

MacAulay, Kelley, and Bobbie Kalman. *Reptiles of All Kinds.* New York: Crabtree, 2005.

O'Neill, Amanda. *I Wonder Why Snakes Shed Their Skin.* New York: Kingfisher, 2003.

Savage, Stephen. *Reptiles: What's the Difference?* Chicago: Raintree, 2000.

Using the Internet

You can explore the Internet to find out more about reptiles. An adult can help you use a search engine. Type in a keyword such as *reptiles* or the name of a particular reptile **species**.

Answer to "Test yourself" question:
A tokay gecko is a reptile.

Glossary

adult grown-up

classification sorting things into groups

communicate send and receive information

crocodilian member of a group of animals that includes crocodiles, alligators, gavials (similar to crocodiles), and caimans (similar to alligators)

embryo very early stage in the growth of an alligator inside its egg

habitat place where an animal lives

incubatation keeping an animal warm

lungs organs that take in air

mate come together to make new animals

nutrient part of food that an animal needs to survive

organ part of an animal's body that has a certain task or tasks

oxygen gas that living things need to survive

predator animal that kills and eats other animals

prey animals that are killed and eaten by other animals

scales bony or horny plates that cover a reptile's skin

skull all the bones of an animal's head

species kind of animal

temperature how warm or cold something is

tropical relating to areas in the world that are warm all year round

webbed with skin between the toes

wetland lake, pond, stream, or swamp

Index